CW00767368

## Self 1

## How to Grow Your Own Food and Live a Self Sustaining Life in the Digital Age

## By Neil M White

The Self Provisioner – Neil M White

This edition first published 2020

Cover Art: Matt Lawrence

**Table of Contents**

# Contents

The Self Provisioner – Neil M White

.

# Foreword – By David The Good

What does self-sufficiency look like?

A man alone, against the world, in a rough cottage of hand-felled pine logs, surrounded by a few acres of crops and a tall, thorny hedge to discourage wandering wildlife?

Sounds lonely to me, though I like the hedge idea.

Maybe your idea of self-sufficiency is having enough money to buy what you want and no one to take away your fridge, your car or your hand-felled pine log cabin if you miss a couple monthly payments.

For years I've contemplated the concept of self-sufficiency and come to the conclusion that it's more of an ideal than an achievable reality, unless you are very clever, healthy and strong, and live in a warm climate with rich soil and abundant rainfall.

White approaches the idea and comes to similar conclusions himself. It's a great idea, it's just not necessarily something we can all make into a reality. Go ahead - produce and set aside as much food as you can. Just don't worry if you can't grow absolutely everything you need. My ancestors grew most of their own food and hunted their own meat for the winter, but they still went to the store to buy sugar and flour.

In Upstate New York, it's rather difficult to grow sugarcane, though I suppose if they were ambitious they could have planted a few acres of sugar maples and then spend their early spring nights in the cold air, boiling cauldrons of sap down into maple sugar...

...but there's that ideal again. You can do it, perhaps, but do you really want to? Do you have to? Do you have to reach a level of perfect purity and have a complete, functioning biodome of a farm where all your possible needs are met?

I don't think so, and neither does White. Instead of being neurotic and attempting to reach the absolute peak of atomistic individuality, where you are a rock, and island, and a sugar baron - you work instead to provide a good amount of food for you and your family, free of poisons and fresher than anything you can purchase.

Some people want everything, right now, all at once. A friend of mine once tried to get me interested in a sketchy off-shore investment that was a "sure thing," and would bring in a lot of money very quickly. I declined and I don't believe he ever had any success with it either. As God reminds us in the book of Proverbs,

*"Wealth gained hastily (or by fraud) will dwindle, but whoever gathers little by little will increase it. (ESV)"*

Many a man has attempted to climb the cliff of "complete" self-sufficiency and found himself half-way up with a slipping rope, plagued by the realization that if he keeps climbing, he may never drink a lager or eat potato chips again... that is, unless he digs another potato bed, finds a way to produce a good frying oil, then travels to the sea to evaporate water for salt... and as for barley and hops...

...and then he falls off the rope, for no normal man can live forever without potato chips, and the complete home production thereof is a Sisyphean task. It is rumored that even Thoreau himself occasionally left Walden and bought himself a can of Budweiser and a bag of Mather's Hot n' Spicy Barbecue Potato Chips.

A wise man knows when to till and when to buy some chips.

In the following book, White takes us down a third path. You will be inspired to stock your freezer with homegrown produce and wild game. You will learn to walk much closer towards self-sufficiency. You will become more resilient and better equipped to deal with the ebb and flow of uncertain economics and political unrest.

Day by day, your savings and your health will increase as you diligently apply yourself to meeting the needs of your family.

One day you may even find yourself growing more food than you can possibly eat.

But if you never make complete self-sufficiency, that's okay as well. It's a dream - not something you have to hit in order to be a success. Success begins with your first home-grown tomato, your first bed of greens, your first venison stew, and it grows from there, like a savings account, bearing interest year after year, until one day you take stock and realize that if need be, you can go for months without visiting the grocery store.

Then you've made it, my friend. You've become a Self-Provisioner.

You don't have to be perfect. You just have to start.

-David The Good, 2020

# Introduction: Everything But the Chicken

This book had humble beginnings. In fact, it started as a photo I shared on the internet. After sitting down to a meal of chicken fillet, beans, peas and potatoes, I realised something cool: everything on my plate had come from my garden.

Everything but the chicken.

That started a cascade of events that started with an idea, turned into a series of blog posts on my blog, ThisDadDoes.com and has culminated in this book. This is the story of how we got to where we are now:

I've written on and off about gardening over the years but as I started to develop this concept it began to make more and more sense to turn it into a book. Like all good books, it started with that small idea - of a plate of food whereas much of it as possible was home grown and sustainably sourced.

Writing on gardening has always come easily. It's easy to write about something you're passionate about. And man, am I passionate about growing stuff. But I'm also a pragmatist and not particularly sentimental. So, I've never seen much point in having a garden that wasn't of practical use. And by use, I mean edible. Which is the way I garden now – primarily focused on growing food.

That's not a new thing for me either. I've been growing vegetables since I was a very young boy – five or six years old. My father even gave me my own plot where I could grow anything (and I mean ANYTHING) I wanted. There aren't many Dads who would do that. The strangest thing we ever tried was a 'walking stick cabbage' that grew to about 7 feet tall. It wasn't edible but you were supposed to be able to make the stalks into walking sticks. When we tried drying the stalks in the garage they rotted and turned to mush.

Then there were a few years when I didn't have a garden. I lived the bachelor life in a Glasgow flat, working and playing a bit too hard. I did grow a pumpkin in a pot in my inner-city apartment to win a bet. Someone in work wagered I couldn't grow a pumpkin in my flat. So, I did and made a pumpkin pie which I then served to the whole office.

A year or so later I was living in Uganda in rural east Africa and grew almost all my own food (with the help of my full-time gardener and mentor, Okethi). Gardening in Africa was easy – you put something in the ground, and it grew – bananas, tomatoes, beans, corn, squash – whatever you wanted, you could grow it. I learned a lot from that old man with a quiet voice and dancing eyes.

Another few years down the line and I read the cult gardening book 'Grow or Die' by David the Good. Before reading this, I'd been fascinated by the idea of growing vegetables for survival. If our world went into meltdown, how would we survive? We'd need food, wouldn't we?

This fascination was compounded by reading further and more widely with writers like Steve Solomon, who invented COF: Complete Organic Fertilizer and others who promote permaculture and 'no-till' types of vegetable growing. Self-sufficiency seemed inviting and romantic. But was it realistic or attainable?

A couple of years after that I got my rifle licence and became a trained deer hunter (you need this in the UK to put venison into the food chain). This added a extra dimension to my 'self provided' diet of vegetables from my plot. Although this book is really about gardening, I'll talk about meat in the last chapter.

Just so you know, there's a full list of all the books I mention in the appendices. I'd recommend reading all of them. You'll learn a lot and understand self provision gardening and where its roots really are.

**Everything But the Chicken – A Journey Away from Self-Sufficiency**

A few years ago, we moved out of the city and into the country. We ended up in a house with plenty of land and I was quick to start growing our own food - potatoes, beans and squash. After my first harvest I was sitting down to a meal of chicken, broad beans (Yanks call these fava beans – I'm not sure why), potatoes and peas. I realised with some surprise that everything, but the chicken had come from my garden.

This was a big moment – a few months earlier when we'd moved into our new house and the garden had been a semi frozen wasteland of mature shrubbery, bark mulch and weeds. Over the following weeks we'd hacked, slashed and dug, bringing a vegetable patch into being through the sweat of our brows.

In this patch of Scottish dirt, I'd grown my first food since leaving Africa seven and a half years before. This plate of chicken and vegetables tasted sweeter than anything I'd eaten. It was the taste of success. So was this 'Everything but the chicken' moment a route on the way to complete self-sufficiency?

My main experience of a self-sufficient lifestyle was through re-runs of the BBC comedy 'The Good Life' in which a young, jet-setting couple left their London city careers to start a self sufficient life in the suburbs. It was hilarious, mainly because they failed at nearly every turn. Now, whenever anyone says 'self sufficiency' that's what I think about. Though I liked the idea of self sufficiency, I knew the reality was near impossible.

Another step in that journey was when I read the gardening and philosophy book by Monty Don (Monty is the slightly eccentric but loveable presenter of BBC's Gardener's World programme). His book, *Down to Earth* was a watershed moment in understanding what I wanted from my garden. Reading the book cover to cover, I came across this quote about the joy and satisfaction of growing your own food:

*"You become nourished by the earth, by your labour, by the intimate and unbroken connection with the ingredients themselves, and by the profound satisfaction of knowing that no one in an office constructed that meal as part of a profit-forecast spreadsheet – let alone used and abused labourers and abased them for a pitiful wage.*

*Whilst self-sufficiency is doomed to humiliating failure, self provision elevates the grower to self-esteem and a world of small but profoundly influential pleasures."*

This phrase 'self provision' stuck in my head. What did it mean? And could you shape an entire lifestyle and philosophy around it? Obviously, I believe you can, that's the whole point of this book. But then if you got this far, you've probably figured that out by now.

Looking back on the months preceding this, I believe I'd been following the 'Self Provision' philosophy without realising it. And certainly, without being able to name it. But how would you define Self Provisioning? Maybe what you're about to read describes how you garden and how you live. If so, that's great. If not, have a think – maybe this is a good way to follow.

The focus of this book is Self Provision Gardening or SPG for short. And we're going to split that idea into broader concepts that I'll elaborate on as the book progresses. But before I do that, I want us to understand what Self Provision Gardening is (and isn't). We're going on this journey together - this book was as much about distilling the essence of SPG as anything.

I should finish this chapter with a vote of thanks to Monty Don who really is one of my gardening heroes. Without him, this book would still be called 'Everything but the Chicken'.

# Chapter 1: What is Self Provision Gardening?

In the introduction, I told you about the idea of Self Provision Gardening. In this chapter I want to explain to you some of the concepts behind this, my gardening philosophy.

I've been actively growing a Self Provision Garden for a while now and have had some great success as well as providing interest for me and my family. Oh, and we grew some delicious, freshalicious fruit and veg.

The thing was, I didn't know I was a Self Provision Gardener until I read '*Down to Earth*' by Monty Don. This got me thinking about what I want or need to get out of my garden. And what guides the way I approach it. So, what is a self provision garden? How does that differ from, say, an ordinary veg plot or garden? And why are we not talking about 'self-sufficiency'? All will be revealed in time. But first…

## 1. A Self Provision Gardener Grows Useful Crops

Imagine you wanted to grow enough food to survive completely self-sufficiently. What would that look like? First up you'd need a lot of land. Living in Uganda I reached the point of near self sufficiency. But I had around three to four acres under cultivation. Even then I bought in difficult to grow staple crops like rice and cassava. Permaculture proponents who believe you can survive on all the vegetables grown in a bathtub sized plot are kidding themselves and you (also that's a quick way to wear out your soil).

*How to Grow More Vegetables* by Jeavons et al is a seminal book on self sufficiency. He does a good job of setting out how exactly you'd go about growing all your nutritional needs. But there is one significant caveat (other than the land you'd need). That is the amount of time you'd need to do this. My demonstration garden in Africa had me as well as a full-time gardener, a part time nursery man (for the tree nursery) and I'd also hire in casual labour for cultivation (all done by hand) and weeding.

In addition, you'd need to keep animals for protein and manure to keep everything fertilised and have crops growing through the year. You would also have to rely on a few high energy crops instead of enjoying a varied and healthy diet. Where I lived in rural Uganda, the local tribespeople ate three main staples –

1. 'Kwen' a stiff porridge made from tapioca flour and water which was then fortified with a little millet or sorghum flour.

2. Beans - a mix of stewed beans in a thick starchy sauce.

3. 'Greens' - kale, cabbage or any other edible leaf.

Sometimes there was a bit of dried fish. And at big celebrations, there was meat. But the focus was on a few dependable, high energy crops.

If you go down the route of self sufficiency, that's where you'd end up - focused on starch root crops and pulses to meet your nutritional needs.

But over here in the Self Provision corner, we're kicking all that idealistic hippy nonsense to the kerb and instead thinking about what fruit and vegetables you *actually* like to eat. That's what I mean by 'useful' – food that you like to eat and cook with. No tapioca or white maize here (unless you love that stuff).

Here's a short list of what I like to eat (and therefore grow):

Cucumbers
Apples
Grapes
Potatoes
Carrots
Figs
Turnip/Swede
Beans
Peas
Asparagus

So if those are the foods you like to eat, and you want to provide for yourself (self provision – geddit?) then you'll want to grow crops you are going to eat, enjoy and build meals around. It's a bit like the circle of life. Or something. Here's how it works:

You like certain kinds of vegetables

You grow those vegetables yourself

You eat those vegetables and enjoy them

Novelty and 'show' crops are out and dependable varieties of heavy cropping, disease resistant veggies are in. If you like to munch them, then they're a keeper. The easier to grow and more suited to your climate the better.

Disease resistance and good breeding is especially important if you're following the 'low input' concept (more on this later). The last thing you want to be doing is buying expensive pesticide chemicals or losing large parts of your harvest to the medium-large hairy Oobit moth (I made this insect up - it doesn't really exist, but Oobit is a Scottish word for caterpillar).

2. A Self Provision Gardener Grows Crops that Store

Knowing what crops store well (and how to store them) is a key part of Self Provision Gardening. Yes we all like to eat salads fresh from the garden, but what do you eat out of season?

Imagine if you could make the produce from your garden last most, if not all of the year? Storing doesn't need to mean freezing or drying either. It might mean root cellaring, canning, pickling or making jams and chutneys. If it makes your abundant harvest last longer so that you are provided for through the autumn, winter and early spring then you are practising self provision.

Crops that are known for storing well are:

Apples
Potatoes
Alliums(onions, garlic)
Root vegetables e.g. carrots

In times gone by, it would have been difficult to learn about preserving food but now with the internet, you can find any number of YouTube tutorials and blogs on the subject. Canning kits or food drying systems can be bought relatively cheaply and, while they might not save you any money, the satisfaction in eating your own preserved food can be hard-to-beat.

Growing crops that store well is a key part of self provision gardening and is what separates us from the casual vegetable grower. Showering regularly is what keeps us apart from the self-sufficiency lot.

## 2. A Self Provision Gardener Uses Minimal Inputs

Sometimes I go to my local garden centre just to be baffled at the range of products, additives and treatments available (orchid compost anyone?) Us Self Provision Gardeners kick all that to the kerb. We're all about using what we've got, minimal inputs including our time and labour. This is about efficiency as well as the satisfaction of growing your own food.

Here are a few ways you can reduce your inputs:

- Make your own compost instead of buying it in or using 'muni-post' – the low-grade recycled stuff which is nutrient destitute.
- Find a source of fresh horse or farmyard manure – even when I lived in the city, the police stables were a 10-minute drive across town so no excuses.
- Grow plants from seed, not ready grown plugs bought from the nursery

- Recycle waste such as wood ash and your own urine for added nutrients.

Another good rule of thumb is making sure that whatever you take off the land in terms of nutrients and carbon is replaced in some way. If you compost all your crop residues, this minimises what is lost from your garden and helps feed the soil for the future.

Inputs can also take the form of expensive tools, compost bins and raised beds. Instead of shelling out big amounts of cash for these things, make do with what you have (most of my tools I've bought cheap, 'borrowed' or acquired when I moved house and found old, abandoned hoes gathering dust in a shed). One of the most pointless additives is 'compost heap activator' which is ammonium sulphite. Bugs love that stuff and it will get your compost pile moving quick style. But what they don't tell you is if you pee on your heap, you'll get the same effect. For free.

## 3. Self Provision is a Way of Living a Better, More Connected Life

In my first book, *A Father's Mission*, I wrote about how we are losing the connection with the land. It's a connection which has lasted millenia but as our farming becomes more and more mechanised and less like actually growing stuff that link is breaking. (I've put this chapter in the appendices of this book for your reading pleasure.)

Self Provision is a realistic way of rediscovering that link. You're not going down the loony road of self-sufficiency which isn't for normies like you and me. But you are going to reach that deep connection with the land and maybe even share that with your children.

Self Provision gardening gives you the joy of growing a meaningful quantity of useful food without the grinding slog of trying to be self sufficient. It is the joy of those sweet new potatoes or crunchy sweet garden peas without the bad back, sunburn or shifty eyes from the neighbours.

## Conclusions

Hopefully I'm making this an easy sell for you. Self Provision Gardening fits in between the casual hobby gardener and the self sufficiency hippy. We love and respect both, but we want to be intentional in the way we garden, but not obsessive.

That's the attraction for me (and hopefully for you) - of realistic and achievable goals, and a lifestyle that is shareable and attractive to others as well as being great for the environment.

# Chapter 2: Choosing a Plot for your Self Provision Garden

If you're looking to start your own Self Provision Garden, there are a few things you need to consider. The most important one is where you are going to site your garden. This can be a challenging question. You might not have enough land. Or maybe your ground is too poor. Or you live in a rented house and don't want to dig up your landlord's lawn to grow veggies.

That's what this chapter is all about. I'm going to give you some ideas for where you can have your Self Provision Garden and start to enjoy the multiple benefits that growing your own food can bring.

I've lived in a range of different places and houses/apartments. I've lived in the inner city of Glasgow where I had no garden or space, just a window (which I made do with). I've also lived in Africa where I had four acres of ground - more than I really knew what to do with. What I do know is that space matters. If you want to do Self Provision Gardening, you are going to need space. You don't need acres of ground. But enough space for three good sized plots (10 x 4 feet each). Why? I'll cover that in a later chapter.

## Say 'No' To Containers if You're Serious

I've got nothing against growing stuff in containers. I do it and I enjoy it. It's useful to be able to more plants around and if I run out of space in the veg patch for a few plants, I can always stick them in pots.

But (and this is a biggie) if you think you'll reach the point of self-provision by having a few plants in pots, you're kidding yourself. Yes you can grow a few potatoes in a bag or pot. And you might get a handful of beans or peas from those grown in a trough. I've had a decent crop of courgettes from pots too.

That's all fun and good interest for your kids. But if you're serious about growing a significant part of your annual veg requirements, then you're going to need a bit more space than a few pots and containers. And if you don't have any space, then you're going to need to find some.

## Space and the Critical Mass

This has nothing to do with astronomy and everything to do with your sanity. Space to grow your food is great - but too much? That becomes a burden. It's better to start with a small area - three 40ft square beds - than a football field.

A garden that is too large is going to leave you discouraged and overburdened. There is no point going down this route if you're going to get stressed about how there's so much to do in the garden and only a few short hours to do it in. That is *not* what self provisioning is all about.

If you start small, you can always work your way up to something bigger. Where I live in Scotland, most gardens are relatively small. I started with a corner of my garden devoted to growing food and expanded over time.

## Use Your Own Space - Start with What You Have

The obvious choice for starting your self provision garden would be to use your own space. If you have a garden or a backyard, you already have a plot of land that you can use. Self Provision Gardening doesn't have to be about using every square inch of your space to grow food.

Old tired bits of grass make really good plots for vegetable and fruit growing. You can use a herbicide to kill the grass off or (for the more patient) black plastic or mulch. My current patch is an old shrubbery which we cleared, composted, manured, dug and now grow great veggies on. In the summer its a really attractive place and backdrop to the garden. But if you don't have any space at home, you could...

## Rent a Space for your Vegetable Garden

Have you considered renting a space to grow food? You could do this in an allotment where you rent a small area of land for veg growing - normally for not very much money. Or you could see if there's a local community food growing centre or garden nearby.

The advantage with these arrangements is that you'll get a secure and extensive area to grow your food. Allotments also put you in contact with other gardeners who are the best source of gardening advice you can find. The disadvantage is that you'll have to travel to the site and either take tools and materials with you or find somewhere to store them on the site. That said, allotments provide a lot of interest and opportunities to learn from others. I even knew an old allotment holder who had an illicit still for making his own rot gut whisky rigged up in his 6 by 4 foot shed.

## Beg, Borrow or Steal a Patch of Ground

OK, so maybe don't steal ground – even 'abandoned' land is normally owned by someone who will care if you turn it into an extension of your garden. But you could go begging around family members, neighbours or friends for a patch of unused garden space. This practice actually has a name - Land Sharing.

The easiest way is land share is to approach someone you know, who lives nearby, and ask if you can use a bit of their ground. It would be good form to offer them some money or a share of the produce as a thank you and for compensation for you showing up at 7.30 in the morning to check the brassicas for caterpillars (just me?). Elderly people are often lonely and find their gardens tough to manage. So, imagine if a young man or woman like you turned up and offered to look after a bit of it for them? If you have family that live nearby you could offer to tend a bit of their garden and share the produce with them.

My parents live nearby and I have an area of their garden for growing my potatoes in. Maincrop potatoes take up a lot of space but don't need much in the way of maintenance or care once they are up and growing so that's perfect for a land share crop.

## Go Big (Enough) or Go Home

If you're serious about self provision gardening, then you will need a bit of space – the more the better. If you've got that at home, great. If not then you'll either need to look at renting a bit of ground or an allotment. Or you could try borrowing some land from friends or family under a land share agreement. Whatever you decide, your solution needs to be of a significant enough size to contribute to your dietary needs.

# Chapter 3: The Low Input Garden

What does it mean to do low input gardening? Is it a realistic way to go about growing your own fruit and vegetables or is it pie-in-the-sky hippy nonsense? That's what I hope to address in this chapter – an approach to gardening which is by definition 'low input'.

The idea of low input gardening is a significant part of Self Provisioning. If you have to rely on loads of chemicals and other inputs to grow your own food, are you really providing for yourself? Anyone can throw a bunch of fertilisers at the ground and end up with big leafy plants and round shiny fruits. The challenge comes when you *minimise* what you put in and still maximise your outputs. We're not going for full self sufficiency here. But we desire to be able to replace some of what you buy in the stores with delicious, homegrown produce.

## What Do I Mean by 'Low Input'?

Gardening with minimal inputs is a foundation concept of self provision gardening. If you need to rely on a whole range of expensive and factory produced chemicals, treatments and pesticides just to make food grow, you're kinda missing the point. In researching for this book, I read an allotment guide by a well-known author. It was full of 'NPK' this and 'spray the bugs' that. Not really what we're talking about here though is it?

I'd be lying if I said I use no chemicals or synthetic fertilisers on my garden. But I don't rely on them and only use as a last resort (i.e. wasp infestations) or as a massive time saver (weed killer on my drive rather than hand pulling weeds for 2 hours every three weeks).

Gardening with minimal inputs is going to take some work and improvisation but it's so much more satisfying eating produce that you know came primarily from hard work, sweat and a fair dollop of ingenuity.

It's also a more sustainable way to live. I'm no eco-warrior but I am tuned into the fact that we only have limited resources on this planet, and we should be thinking about using less wherever we can. It might not matter to you, but it will to your children or their children. Who is to say that our relative period of abundance that we enjoy now will last forever?

A low input garden is all good, but it should also be a low output garden in terms of generating waste. All of your garden wastes and harvesting residues should go back into the garden (as much as is possible). Anything you can't compost can be burned or used as mulch. In my neighbourhood, we have a green waste collection by the local authority. But I rarely put garden wastes in the bin at all. Everything that is 'waste' produced by the garden can be composted or used in some way.

When I have woody sticks and stems, I let them dry by the compost heap and then burn once or twice a year. The ash goes back into the compost heap or can used as fertiliser for fruit trees. The potash will encourage big, healthy fruits.

I don't apply this strictly – a big part of self provision gardening is being realistic (not idealistic). I have a big hedge around my house and garden and the amount of clippings this produces is colossal – far more than my small-ish veg patch could cope with. Some of it goes to the municipal tip for making into compost there.

## How You Can Incorporate Low Inputs into Your Garden

So how do you actually do low input gardening? I'm not going to lie to you and say it's the easiest way or that it will give you the most vegetables per square foot. But what I will say is that it is satisfyingly sustainable giving you scrumptious sundries for all. Here's how you can do it:

## 1. Make Your Own Compost

This is the simplest way to practice low input gardening. If you're on the path to self-provision then a big part of that is compost. Think about it this way – you are making new soil. It doesn't get more 'self providing' than that.

Compost doesn't have to be complicated – nature does it all the time. I'm pretty lazy when it comes to compost. I just pile everything in a big heap and let nature do its thing (more on this in the next chapter. My compost includes:

All non meat/bread food waste
Urine

Human hair
Gardening residues
Grass clippings
Coffee grounds
Animal manures

Pretty much anything that isn't going to be a biohazard when it rots and will give me rich, high organic matter-based compost goes on there. My smallish garden creates around a cubic metre of compost in a year - plenty of new organic matter which is food for all the bugs that live in your soil.

## 2. Work with Nature, Not Against It

This is a principle to live by in the garden. Think about it this way – nature is pretty much self sustaining when we're not interfering. If you spray pesticides everywhere or rip out all the wildflowers for miles around you will do several things:

1. Kill every living, crawling and flying thing in a significant area.
2. Bump off beneficial insects as well as those that munch your crops.
3. Don't deny bees and other pollinators food and sustenance.

Here's something that's really easy to do: make your garden a bit messy (I have three kids so it does this all on its own). Don't manicure everything or clear up every last dead leaf and twig. Beneficial animals and bugs love this stuff. I've seen toads, hedgehogs and more ladybirds than I can count – all of which are a vegetable gardeners friend.

This also means not fighting against the seasons. If you have to grow all your crops under cloches, fleece or start every seedling in the greenhouse then you are fighting with nature, not working with it.

Crop choice (I'll come on to this) really matters as well as selecting the right varieties for your location. Which brings me on to….

## 3. Be Prepared to Experiment

I was speaking to a gardening friend of mine who was complaining about eelworm in their potatoes and carrot flies in their carrots. I didn't have either this year. Why? Because I bought a variety of eelworm resistant potato and a type of carrot called 'Resistafly' – self explanatory I hope.

Sure I could have nuked the soil with additives and put up barriers to stop carrot fly. But it's easier to grow crops that aren't affected. Heritage varieties of veg are fun to grow – but they've often fallen out of fashion because of major weaknesses in breeding or susceptibility to pests.

I've also tried to do more with fleeces and netting to stop pests getting to my veggies. It's not going to give you complete protection, but it does work.

Another approach is what I call 'Give the Birds a Third'. This means that you mentally write off a third of your crops to pests like birds and other thieves. That way you'll avoid the sense of loss when they eat your stuff. If you end up with more, you've won.

## 4. Don't Overcrop Your Land

A lot of permaculture guides and gurus will tell you how to have your ground at peak production for ten months of the year. That's a cool idea and will sell you lots of books or get your loads of attention on the internet when you post photos of all the foot you grew from four square feet of land. But in the real world, your garden needs time to recover and rest. Just because you can crop your garden year-round doesn't mean you should.

Traditional farming has always included fallow periods to let the ground rest and recover. If you don't like the look of bare soil, try some green manures like mustard or rye grass (read on for more on this).

## 5. Saving Your Own Seed

One of my favourite characters in the book and movie *'The Big Short'* is Ben Rickett - a quirky ex-Wall Street veteran and prepper who believes that the future world's currency will be seeds once the economy has crashed and gone to the dogs. Maybe he'll turn out to be right yet?

Seeds are about as important for our survival as a species as you can imagine. So important that most developed countries have banks where seed can be stored near indefinitely. One of the most well-known of these is the Svalbald Global Seed Vault which is on a Norwegian island close to the North Pole (I'm not making this up!). There are over 400,000 species and varieties stored at Svalbald. If the zombies ever break into there and get a taste for kernels, we're toast.

But if you don't want to rely on the Scandinavians for protecting your seed resource, you could always store your own. Seeds need to be nice and cool and dry - keeping them in a refrigerator is ideal. Alternatively an airy garage or shed will do just as well.

## 6. Use Deep Mulches to Suppress Weeds and Improve Fertility

Deep mulching is a technique popularised in Ruth Stouts *'Gardening Without Work'*. She writes extensively about how she covers her whole plot in a layer of thick mulch and has a strict 'no dig' policy on her beds.

What you use isn't important - spoiled hay, wood chips, grass clippings - all are organic and make a thick covering which will break down slowly.

My take on this involves recycling waste and improving your garden while reducing weeds **all at the same time.** I take all my old cardboard boxes (plain, undyed is best) and lay them flat on the soil and cover with a coating of my own compost. The cardboard stops weeds coming through while the compost will rot down eventually and worms and other organisms will incorporate it into the soil, improving the structure. That's an ultimate low input way to eliminate weeds.

## Give Low Input Gardening a Go

This isn't an exhaustive list of ideas or things you can do to lower the inputs into your garden.

But it does give you an idea of what we're talking about. Next time you plan a trip to the garden centre, stop yourself and think 'Is there another way I could do this?'

Gardening with low inputs is the most satisfying way you can garden. If you know that your produce was grown with the minimum of additives and outside assistance, they will taste that much sweeter - like victory.

# Chapter 4: All About Compost

You don't get something for nothing these days. There's no such thing as a free lunch. Or is there? This chapter is all about one of my favourite topics: Compost.

Thinking about what was going to go in this chapter was a bit daunting. There have been so many books written covering the subject of composting that it feels a bit precocious to try and add anything. I really recommend checking out Steve Solomon's work on the subject *Gardening When it Counts* as well as David The Good's book - *Compost Everything*. Both of these really challenged what I thought I knew about the subject - For a full further reading list, check out the appendices.

I suppose the only way to really approach this subject is to go fully from my own experience. I'm not going to go through the different types of composting (hot/cold?) or the types of heaps because this information is elsewhere. I'm going to assume that you're reading this with a basic understanding of the concept of compost but if not, here's a super quick rundown of the (slightly smelly) facts.

## What is Compost?

Nature makes compost every day and has done for a long time. Stuff dies, falls to the ground, gets eaten and poo-ed out. That poo is then broken down by bacteria and other organisms and eventually becomes hummus - the organic component of ordinary soil. That's composting.

But this book isn't about going into the woods and digging up forest soil to sprinkle on your garden - don't do this. If we're going to provide food for ourselves, we're going to make our own hummus. Oh, and we're going to do it quicker than nature on its (her?) own.

Most compost heaps in garden situations are made of a mix of kitchen scraps and garden waste. Some also contain 'special' additives which we'll cover later in this chapter. This mix eventually breaks down to something resembling hummus that can then be spread on your garden.

## Why Compost?

Back when we were digging for victory, or even earlier when people plain ol' grew stuff to survive, everyone had a compost heap. It wasn't always called that but there was one. Part of this was necessity - if you had a garden, you needed somewhere to put all the waste that wouldn't burn. Municipal garden waste collection is a new thing. Before that, we pretty much all composted.

It's simple really - compost is a convenient and sustainable way to recycle your garden and kitchen waste. For us self provision gardeners, that's a big part of what we're about - low inputs and using what we have. I see compost a bit like the old pseudo-science of alchemy which aimed at turning lead into gold. Instead of the perpetually unsuccessful attempts, composting is a roaring success nearly every time. All you need to do is:

1. Collect garden waste, kitchen scraps and anything else that is biodegradable (shredded paper, old cardboard, roadkill, human urine) and pile it in a big heap.
2. Aim for a 50/50 split of green, leafy material to brown, woody stuff.
3. Pile it up and leave for several months
4. Turn it you feel like it. If not, put the kettle on and have a cup of tea instead.

After a period of time, what was horrible half rotten kitchen scraps, slimy garden waste and dry grasses will have turned into humus - lovely, rich smelling humus which is now ready to mix into your garden soil.

## What Does Compost Do?

What most gardeners don't realise is that ordinary garden compost is fairly low in nutrients compared to manures and other organic fertilisers. Which is why I don't see compost as food for plants. Instead its food for the soil.

Soil might seem like dead stuff but actually it's alive alive-o with billions of bacteria and tiny little bugs. They eat the compost and poo out nitrogen which your plants can then enjoy. The organic matter in the compost also helps condition your soil so it's not worn out. This helps with drainage, water retention and can even keep your soil from freezing solid.

You can dig it into the soil or lay it on top as a mulch. Or a bit of both. If you have worn out soil with low organic matter, I'd suggest laying a thick layer of the stuff on the surface. Worms will incorporate it into the soil over time while the mulch will protect the soil from wind and water erosion.

Visiting a no till demonstration farm in Lesotho, Southern Africa, I saw first-hand the power of mulch. There the rich volcanic soils are high in minerals but low in organic matter and are easily washed away. The farmer showed me how a thick layer of mulch helped protect the soil by pouring a big bucket of water on it. The mulch protected the soil and the water soaked in with minimal run-off.

## How to Build a Compost Heap

There is a whole economy out there based on trying to sell you contraptions for making compost. Which would be funny if it wasn't such a scam. You don't need fancy plastic, purpose built containers or any of that stuff. You don't even need a container.

My compost heap at my farm in Uganda was just a few sharpened sticks in a square to keep things tidy. My first heap at the house I live in now was just a heap of stuff in the middle of a patch of dirt.

But if you want to keep things a bit tidier, you could make an easy heap out of a few bits of old wood and chicken wire. Check out *How to Grow More Vegetables* by Jim Jeavons for some really useful designs. His self-supporting chicken wire design could be made for the cost of a bit of wire netting and a scrap of sawn timber.

There is a load of inspiration on the internet too. A simple search with give you hundreds of ideas. My first heap cost me around £11.00 which was a box of screws and a few bits of wood. My second - a bit sturdier - was around £38.00 but that was for two heaps. I used old bits of timber I'd salvaged from my Dad's garden and bits of an old shipping pallet.

Some compost advocates tell you to build the compost heap in layers - a layer of this, a layer of that. But for me it takes me a full year to fill one of my compost heaps. So layering is out of the question. As things become available, they get chucked on the heap. However, there are a few things to consider when taking this approach:

Pay attention to the 'browns/greens' rule. Aim for a 50-50 split. If you've got too much 'greens' (I find this during the winter when all I have it kitchen scraps and coffee grounds), add some woody material like dried grass, straw or shredded leaves. This stops your heap going manky and smelly.

Too much 'browns' will have the opposite effect: a difficult to digest lump of woody, dry material that won't resemble compost for years.

If you end up with too much of one type of material, put it to the side and mix it in gradually. I like to do this with spent potting compost which is excellent 'browns'.

Turn and mix if you like, but not too much. For one, this is a lot of work for not much benefit. I'm not a hot composter (hot compost is where the heap is manipulated to produce compost in a matter of weeks) - one good load of compost per year does my whole garden so speed isn't of the essence.

OK, so you've made your compost. What do you use it for? First up, compost is not a replacement for animal manures - it just isn't that high in nitrogen. The best way to use garden compost is as an organic matter additive to your soil. Bugs in your soil love (and I mean LOVE) organic matter. It's their favourite thing to eat.

And when they eat that organic matter, they poo. And that poo contains nitrogen that is either eaten by other bugs (yuk) or taken up directly by plants. Plants need nitrogen to grow healthily and produce fruit. The more nitrogen they can get, the happier they are.

When you harvest crops from an area, add a few shovelfuls of your own compost, some animal manure and wood ash and mix into the soil. This will enrich the soil, replacing nutrients that have been lost.

Everyone knows that food wastes and garden residues make good compost. But there are a few other items that can be composted but won't ever be talked about on BBC's Gardener's World. Read on...if you dare!

**Five Weird Things You Didn't Know You Could Compost**

Before we go further, let me give you fair warning that if you are a bit squeamish, this isn't the section for you. Maybe skip to the next chapter or take up flower arranging. I'm not saying you need to follow these next few steps to be a Self Provision Gardener. However, if you want to be fully ready for a Mad Max/Waterworld style global meltdown and have a kick-ass garden at the same time, read on.

I also can't take full credit for these ideas. Most of my 'experimental' attitude to the compost heap came from David the Good's book *Compost Everything*. All of the following items have ended up on my compost at some stage.

**1. Human Urine**

I recently picked some of my own plums and took them round to a friend. After trying one, they asked me if I used any fertiliser.

'Only my personal special blend.' I said, innocently.

They'll never know (unless they read this of course) that I was talking about my own wee. Recently I've come to see our pee as one of the most underused resources. We produce gallons of it every month. And then flush it down the loo where it mixes with poo and creates toxic waste which we then spend millions to 'treat' before releasing it into the ocean. So is there a better way? Imagine if you could recycle that so-called waste product.

The problem is that urine on it's own is too 'hot'. It contains too much nitrogen to be useful to your plants and could harm them instead.. So you need to mix it with organic matter to dilute it a bit.
Enter the compost heap. Most gardeners have a problem with too much carbon based organic matter (browns) and not enough nitrogen based stuff (greens)  So adding a litre or so of your own pee every now and then is a very good idea. It will also help keep the heap moist in dry weather.

The nitrogen in your urine will have two effects. Firstly it will speed up the composting process, giving the bugs in there something to get them going and working through the carbon material. It will also enrich the heap as the nitrogen content of the whole will increase giving you better quality compost.

To save your urine, try collecting it in a milk bottle. Or you could 'go' on the heap – as long as the neighbours aren't watching…

For a guide on how to make an outdoor urinal/urine composter, check out the appendices.

## 2. Human Hair

Confession time: I used to think my mother was a raving lunatic for putting hair clippings on the compost. But did you know hair is a source of nitrogen for your compost?

I cut my hair at home as do my wife and daughter. Rather than put the clippings in the bin, I put them straight onto the compost. I'm not only reducing the household waste but I'm feeding The Heap at the same time.

If you want to take things a step further, make friends with your local barber for a free, regular supply (provided this is legal where you live, it's not everywhere). You could also use pet hair if you have an abundant supply of that.

## 3. Leftover Beer and Wine

Yes, that is an actual thing (or so I've been told). Here's the thing: sometimes you have guests over and you open 2 bottles when one would have done. Now you've got half a bottle of white left and your other half is watching her figure while you've gone sober for October. So what do you do with the leftovers? Pour down the sink? Feed to the neighbours cat? (don't do this)

Put them on the compost of course!

Yes wine and beer contain alcohol but they also contain a lot of sugar which is like a prime buffet for the bugs who make your compost so yummy for plants. The neighbours will think you've lost it, but then they already caught you weeing on the garden at eleven o'clock in the morning. This is nothing. You can also put leftover beer on the heap but I've never had any of that so you would need to try it for yourself.

## 4. Used Coffee Grounds

Pretty much since the age of twelve, I've drank between two and seven strong cups of coffee per day. I have an espresso machine, a French press and a percolator espresso thingy – sometimes they all get used on the same day. This coffee addiction (let's call a spade 'a spade') produces a large amount of leftover coffee grounds.

But did you know that used coffee grounds have a similar nutrient profile to animal manures? And if you put that waste coffee in the bin rather than the compost, you're wasting a big opportunity, not to mention contributing to a global waste problem.

Instead, gather it together in a bin (I just mix it with the veg peelings and leftovers from breakfast) and dump on the heap when full. If you want to take things further, you could scam the grounds from the office coffee machine or even trawl your local cafes looking for used coffee. Make sure you mix this with plenty of carbon-based material i.e. 'browns' to stop it going all rancid.

Something to bear in mind is that coffee grounds are quite acidic so if you're using a lot or collecting from local cafes, you'll need some way of balancing that acidity out. Which leads us on to number five….

## 5. The Bottom of the Barbeque

OK, so I don't mean that cremated sausage that fell through the grill and stayed there, slowly going blacker and blacker until it was unrecognisable. Oh no! I'm talking about….. wood ash! Ash has been used as a soil improver for thousands of years. It contains essential minerals that your plants need to grow and thrive. So, don't throw any of it out unless it's on the garden.

As well as your own wood ash, you could try collecting your neighbours' or family members' ash. I get my parents to save the ash from their wood burning stove for my heap although I suspect they keep some for themselves too.

If you have a bonfire, keep the ash and spread on your heap in a fine layer. Little chunks of charcoal are good too as they absorb nutrients and water which will help your soil in the long run. Just be careful of burning plastics or coated papers – you don't really want those chemicals in your soil.

## A Word on No-Till and Mulches

I'm not convinced that this needs a chapter all of its own. I've not really done no till gardening though I saw it well practiced in Lesotho, Southern Africa.

I've read widely on the subject and there a few things to consider for the two systems. Both no till and mulch-based gardening are similar and have interchangeable parts (mulch garden purists do almost no digging). However 'no till' doesn't mean 'no work'.

## No Till Gardening

The project I visited in Southern Africa was built around the concept of Conservation Agriculture. This meant working with nature and the soil rather than trying to tame it like a wildly behaved child. Crop residues were left to decay naturally, ploughs were banned, and water conservation was top priority.

The success of this system was plain to see as we travelled through the small kingdom passing barren and eroded fields. Eventually we came to a fast-flowing river and piled into a row boat (the ferry) to cross. What we entered was like a paradise - green fields, smiling, healthy people, orchards and food. In a country that still relied on US food aid, these people were **selling their surplus** to the aid programme to then be distributed to their neighbours. They could then send their children to school and rent more ground to farm and conserve.

Conservation gardening depended on minimal ground disturbance, using mulches and targeted fertilising and crop spacing to increase yields exponentially. It was working big time.

**Mulch Gardening**

This is different to No Till in that you cover the ground with a thick layer of mulch which breaks down over time, suppresses weeds and feeds the soil. It also insulates the soil which, in theory, should give you better growth rates and germination. Authors like Ruth Stout (see *Gardening without Work*) would have you believe that this technique is easy street. But after a bit of digging, the truth is that you need two things:

A ready supply of mulch material - spoiled hay, spent mushroom compost, cardboard, grass clippings, tree residues. Or…

Loads of time to collect prolific quantities of 1.

The problem with this is that it's not exactly 'low input' and outwith the principles of Self Provisioning. If you need to buy in trailer loads of mushroom compost or other organic materials to grow your food, you don't have a sustainable system for growing your own food. There, I said it!

**My Take:**

Like most philosophies with die hard followings, both No Till and Mulch Gardening have value in their techniques. My approach is to take the principles and incorporate into my own gardening style by:

Doing minimal digging and tillage of the soil. Once your beds are light and fluffy and have plenty of organic matter in them, there is little to be gained by deep or double digging. You'll just bring subsoil to the surface that has little benefit for your plants.

Using mulches liberally. This includes my own compost, well-rotted horse manure from the nearby organic livery, cardboard and shredded hedge trimmings. I try to leave these to rot on the surface as much as possible and let earthworms (nature's earth movers) do their thing.

Regular hoeing of the soil. This was something I witnessed in Uganda and Lesotho. Weeds were hoed regularly until crops could outcompete or were ready to harvest. Often, they were left on the soil in the sun to wilt and decompose. You can do this on a sunny day or by laying them out on a path to die before putting in the compost heap (avoid weed seeds though). A stirrup or Dutch hoe will do the job nicely.

## Compost is Alchemy

Alchemy was the old pseudoscience of turning lead into gold. Enthusiasts believed that if they could just crack the code, they would be able to turn ugly lumps of soft metal into gleaming, valuable gold. Of course, it was impossible. But there is a form of alchemy that works. It's called composting.

Think about it: you take all your kitchen scraps, weeds, rubbish, gardening waste, human hair, urine (ew!) and wood ash. You mix it together a bit, leave it for a bit (longer the better) and it turns into wonderful, rich compost that you can use to grow more plants. Never let this miracle lose it's magic. You might not have gold, but then you can't grow food in gold anyway.

# Chapter 5: A Year in the Self Provision Garden

A garden is a year-round commitment. While there might be times of the year that you're less busy in the garden, there are still jobs to do, crops to plan and things to buy for the coming season. In seasonal climates, gardening follows a natural pattern. Stuff doesn't grow in the middle of winter. Which is great because you probably don't want to spend too much time out there anyway. In many countries, winter is the main time for hunting and so an opportunity to stock up on meat. More on this in a later chapter.

I prefer to work with nature and the natural rhythm of the seasons. Yes you can cover your garden in black plastic, warm the soil and steal a march in, well March, and get your potatoes in early. But this flies in the face of what we're trying to achieve - sustainable, low input garden that is still productive. If you try to subdue the natural process, seasons then eventually you'll lose.

All seasons have a natural pace and beat to them. As the birds and insects start to wake up in the spring, so does the garden. It breathes for the first time and the smells fill your nostrils - decaying leaves, spring blossoms and wet grass are the best signals that it will soon be time to plant.

Summer brings the heady heat, long evenings and early harvest of peas, green beans and other crops. You'll taste the first new potatoes and lift your root crops. Summer salads, barbeques and al fresco dining making self provision gardening that much more enjoyable.

Autumn brings the last of the harvest and when you'll store crops, save seed for next year and prepare your garden for the winter months ahead. The last few warm days bring beautiful sunsets and fresh, crisp mornings.

Winter is not a holiday for the self provision gardener. Instead you'll be tidying, planning for next year and buying seeds and plants. Oh and you'll also be harvesting winter crops right through until the weather starts to turn warmer.

As the soil dries and the temperature climbs, sowing time beckons. Watch what farmers are doing. They know the natural beat of the calendar better than anyone. For the self provision gardener, spring is when it really starts. So that's where I'm going to start.

## Spring

You've made it through the long, cold and dark winter months. As the birds start to chirrup and the temperature warms, you know what's coming next: spring. And spring means one thing - gardening.

Spring is easily the busiest time for the self provision gardener. You'll be working against the clock to get all your crops sown, beds prepared, and compost spread. The work that you put in autumn and winter will have lasting benefits - the manure and compost has broken down and rotted so that its nearly indistinguishable from the soil. If you are starting a self provision garden from scratch, you'll really get going in spring.

## 1. Form or reform your growing beds.

While timber edged raised beds are all the rage just now (and do have some advantages), I like Steve Solomon's compromise of semi-raised beds. These are raised above the surrounding ground level by around 15cm (6 inches) but don't have sides made out of wood or brick as popular raised beds do. This saves on the cost and also preserves water in your beds. Wooden boards wick moisture away from plant roots. Wood is porous and absorbent. Save the money and improve your yields at the same time.

The ideal dimension for a semi raised bed is 1.2m (4 feet) by however long you need it to be. Unless you have a massive garden or field, this will be around 8-9 metres max (25 feet). This gives you 100 square feet in one bed which is perfect in size for whatever you want to grow. I'd suggest having at least three of these so that you can do crop rotation.

Once these beds are formed, you can keep them as semi-permanent features. You will need to reform them each year as the constant working of the soil will change the shape. You will inevitably tread the edges making them slightly smaller than they should be. Each spring, measure them, adjust the size and reform them. I'd recommend reading Steve Solomon's book '*Gardening when it Counts*' for more details on this technique.

## 2. Dig out your compost heap.

We've already established that composting is a good thing to do, really good for the environment and turns your household waste into soil. So I'm not going to rehash that info here. But spring is an important time for the compost heap if, like me, you take the slow 'cold' composting approach. This means letting your heap slowly decompose and cure over winter. Come spring, your compost will be ready to use.

Remove the cover (old carpet is good for this) and start to dig away. You'll probably come across un-rotted food and woody debris. Just toss these in next year's heap and everything will be well rotted come next year.

Use the compost for adding organic matter back into your beds, as mulch or sift and use as a potting mix. My own compost comes out quite 'rough' but it's great for mulches and as a soil improver. Compost which is made with a lot of coffee grounds - like mine - will be quite acidic so you could add lime or wood ash to sweeten it.

## 3. Plant (but don't go crazy).

When I say, 'don't go crazy', what I mean is this: It's far too tempting as a new self provision gardener to go rushing in, trying to grow everything in your first year. Instead, try a few different crops (four or five is perfect) and see how it works out. If it's good, do that again next year plus some new crops or varieties. You'll save yourself a lot of stress by following this approach and probably have better results too.

My gardening hero David The Good suggests just growing root crops to begin with. If you can grow potatoes, carrots, swede then you'll be able to grow trickier crops. A useful starting list would be:

Potatoes

Kale

Pumpkin/squash

Broad beans

Peas

These are all high energy, high nutrient crops which store well and are relatively easy to grow.

If you can make these work, vary the theme. If you like these crops, stick with them (all of these stores well either dried, in the cellar/garage or frozen so are great for self provision gardening).

Remember, self provision gardening is about growing crops to replace things that you'd normally buy (or aren't able to buy) for a significant part of the year. This becomes harder if you have three types of bean, four different varieties of pumpkin and eight types of lettuce on the go at one time.

## Summer

Your enjoyment of the garden in summer will depend on how organised you were during the previous two seasons. Did you plan and prepare properly. Was your crop choice on point. Did you get everything planted on time and in the right place?

If you did all that then guess what? You get to relax and enjoy the garden a little. I like to sit in my pergola, coffee in one hand, cigar or my pipe in the other while the summer sun sinks slowly behind my beech hedge. In the distance you can hear the gentle hum of bees as they do your work for you. Here are some other jobs to keep you going over the summer months.

## 1. Summer pruning and harvesting

One of the joys of summer is fresh, ripe fruits. Sun warmed and picked straight from tree to mouth - is there anything finer? Keep on top of your harvesting. Some plants like peas and beans need you to be on top of picking to keep crops of pods coming. Runner beans will 'go over' if you don't do this. The pods become leathery and inedible and you'll have to wait until the pods mature to harvest the dried beans. Asparagus needs regular picking - a large patch needs daily attention. Fruit trees such as apples may need summer pruning to remove vigorous growth and stimulate future fruit production.

## 2. Weed, Weed, Weed

You know you else likes summer? Weeds, that's who. Those little rascals will grow in the hottest, driest weather. Or they wait for a nice damp humid spell to explode into seeds giving you work for weeks to come. The trick with weeding is simple - little and often. Take your stirrup hoe on your daily rounds of your garden and give the surface a little tickle. This has two functions:

1) It will cut off the roots of any weeds, disturbing them and killing them. The morning is best for this as the warm summer sunshine will stress and kill the plant.
2) Disturbing the top layer of soil and 'fluffing' it creates a barrier that prevents excessive water loss. You should do this after heavy rain as a matter of course.

## Autumn

Autumn is when you will harvest many of your crops – especially winter storage crops. But that doesn't have to end with empty beds, and a winter of cleaning up leaves and fallen twigs. Instead you could be using that time to plan for next year, prepare and feed your soil and even steal a march on next year's harvest.

I live in east Scotland which means quite strong winds, short days and long, mild winters. That gives a bit of flexibility in terms of what I can grow. And it's perfect for self provisioning. Why? Because the main energy crops (think starchy veggies) and nutritious greens (kale and other cabbage family) grow great through much of the year.

So what jobs can a self provision gardener be doing during the autumn season?

## 1. Plan for Next Year

Once the dust settles on this year's harvest and everything you need is in storage for the winter, you have the chance to sit down and plan for next year. Ask yourself these questions:

What went well – what worked. And most importantly, what didn't?

What crops will go where next year? It's important to rotate your crops to give the soil a break and stop harmful diseases building up in the soil - follow legumes and fruit crops with potatoes/roots and follow them with brassicas (cabbage family) then back to the start.

What are you going to try that's new?

I like to sit down with a notepad and paper and plan out my beds. The slight lull in the gardening calendar means you can also spend some time shopping around and researching varieties of vegetables that will enjoy your climate.

For me, anything tender or frost sensitive is out (unless very quick maturing) as parts of Scotland can have frosts right into May.

## 2. Rehabilitate and Prepare Your Soil

If you are developing a self-provision garden, then this should mean minimal inputs. I don't use any synthetic fertilisers on my veggie patch and try to only use what nature gives. This means a number of things:

- Compost which I make myself.
- Animal manures from local stables or farms. Horse is good. One year I got some alpaca manure which is supposed to be good sh*t.
- Green manures – legumes, mustard and buckwheat are good autumn/winter growing varieties.
- My own urine which I 'dilute' in the compost heap or outdoor urinal (see the appendix for details on how to make your own one of these).

If you grow crops for food, your soil is the most valuable thing you've got. As someone wise said 'your wealth is in the soil'. Imagine the soil like a bank account – if all you ever make is withdrawals; you're going to run out of cash soon. Same with your dirt – don't get into debt. Put back at least as much as you took out.

Autumn is a great time to do this. The long winter season will allow your manures and mulches to rot and be broken down so that when spring comes, you can just dig them in and plant away.

## 3. Plant Overwintering Crops

I'm not a big fan of 'Permaculture' as the concept of using every spare inch of soil all the time, all year round just screams UNSUSTAINABLE IN THE LONG TERM at me.

But that doesn't mean I won't touch overwintering crops. Self Provision Gardening is about finding what works and then doing it over and over until you're really good at it. That will mean a few failures but that's fine if you learn something from it.

Much of the decision making about overwintering crops is made for me in that the climate here in East Scotland is pretty inhospitable for things to grow through it. However, alliums (onions, garlic) will grow well through winter. Other 'autumn' crops such as broad beans tend to do less well.

## 4. Go Foraging

Foraging - where you gather free food from forests or hedgerows - dates back to the early days of mankind. Hunter-gatherers have been doing this for thousands and thousands of years. And you'd be surprised how much free food is out there.

Near where I live, we can gather plums, brambles, gooseberries and mushrooms all for free. A word of warning - don't eat mushrooms unless you know exactly what they are and always get the landowners permission before going gathering.

In short, autumn is one of my favourite times of year. It feels like change and the chance for new beginnings. Some of the coolest and best things in my life have happened in the season before winter. I love getting out into the garden as the days start to shorten, pick the last of the harvest and get the garden ready for the next year.

## Winter

Winter can be a long and depressing time for the gardener. One of the things I struggle with the most is not really seeing the garden. We become like strangers as the days shorten. I leave the house in darkness and return after nightfall. I might catch glimpses of the garden during the weekends - if I'm lucky and the weather isn't too bad.

But that doesn't mean you're off the hook when it comes to your garden. There are still lots of things to be doing during those long, cold weeks. Here are some jobs to be doing in your 'off season'.

## 1. Get stuck into a building project

Over the last two winters, I've built three compost heaps as well as a leaf composter. The dark, cold days mean that it's much more attractive to stay indoors and work on something in the garage. A few years ago, I picked up a space heater when my office was having a clear out which is perfect for doing a bit of indoor self provisioner construction.

It's perfectly reasonable to leave these kinds of projects to the winter. I've also constructed beds for fig trees and used the winter to clear scrub and woody shrubs to make way for more vegetables. You won't be spending time weeding or pruning, so make the time count on things that are going to get jettisoned when the warmer days and longer evenings beckon.

## 2. Order seeds and crops for spring

Like clockwork, seed catalogues start appearing in your letter box in early January. While I buy my seeds mainly online and from a local trusted garden centre, I still love to flick through the glossy pages of the seed catalogue for inspiration. You should already have a plan of what to grow and where - remember to rotate your crops in the following rough order: fruit crops and legumes > potatoes and root crops > brassicas.

Some seed suppliers will take your whole order and then drip feed you the products, tubers and seeds as they are needed. This is good for the impatient sort like me and means you get lots of exciting packages in the mail. The only problem I find with this is that often these companies are based in the South of England where the climate is much more favourable. I get my potatoes two weeks to a month before I really need them!

## 3. Plant overwintering root and bulb crops

Did you know some crops actually need the cold depths of winter to grow? Alliums (garlic, onions etc) need cold temperatures to do well. There are early varieties of garlic and onions that have been bred specifically to do well sitting in the cold.

These will mature much faster than spring planted varieties as they've had all winter to establish and put down roots (they'll grow albeit slowly). Other 'later' varieties of onions and garlic can be planted in January or February provided that the soil isn't waterlogged.

The trick is not to plant these into cold, wet soil. You'll find your success rate is vastly decreased if you do this. I once planted some asparagus crowns into horrible wet soil and had a big disappointment. If you can, wait until the soil is a little dry and certainly not frozen. Doing this will greatly increase your success rate. You could cover with fleece to keep off the worst of the northern European weather. A little trick is to also raise some bulbs in root trainers or small pots in a garage or sheltered spot. These can then be used to fill any gaps that appear in your allium beds.

## 4. Go Hunting

In a lot of places - Scotland included - winter is the main time for hunting. Not many above ground animals rear young during the winter and so mammals and birds are more likely to be in season. Meat doesn't spoil hanging in a cold garage the same way it would in spring or summer. If you have a hunting ground or know someone who does, take the opportunity to fill up the freezer.

## Final Thoughts

Wherever you live, the seasons have a natural rhythm. Where I lived in the semi-arid equatorial climate, people lived (and died) by the timing of the two rainy seasons - one long and one short. Here in western Europe, growing food is more about getting enough done in the spring and summer to make harvesting in late summer, autumn and even winter profitable.

My biggest lesson has been not to fight the seasons. Rather than trying to resist nature, work with the seasons and times. You will grow and gather more food in the same amount of time with less effort and fewer inputs.

# Chapter 6: All About Meat

When I started writing this book, I never planned to write about meat. I was going to call the book 'Everything but the chicken' because I think (for most people) having your own livestock or poultry is unrealistic. Self provisioning is meant to be realistic and attainable - not pie-in-the-sky hippy dippy 'make your own clothes from plant fibres' nonsense.

Right up to this point you'd be thinking this is a gardening book. And you'd be right: most of this book is about gardening and growing your own food. So how does meat fit into this picture?

I will answer that question in full. But right now I want you to imagine…

## Imagine A World Where Meat is Scarce

Can you imagine that? I can. I lived it for nearly a year. In rural Uganda where I lived for most of 2008 there was limited refrigeration and meat was expensive - one kilo of beef was three dollars. This was 4 days wages for a manual worker. Most people never saw meat in a shop. Cattle were butchered early morning at the side of the road and carved up by mid-morning to prevent spoiling. It was cooked that day - normally long and slow in a stew.

Goat could be dry cured in the rafters of the 'kitchen' - a mud hut with grass roof which filled completely with smoke during mealtimes. Sometimes the curing process was incomplete, the flavour was a mix of wood smoke and cadaver.

Chickens were eaten occasionally - normally when there was something to celebrate. Fish was more common. But what people in my village really waited for was...

TERMITE SEASON.

A couple of times a year, winged termites would swarm. These could be harvested with a lamp and a plastic basin. As night fell, the termites emerged and were attracted to the light. As they tired, they would fall to the ground and could be collected up. The termites were de-winged and then eaten in a variety of ways:

- Fresh - think 'still alive'
- Dry roasted (pretty good)
- Ground into meat balls (very filling, not so good)
- Made into paste with shea oil (this was considered the food of royalty and with good reason - my favourite).

In a place where animal protein was scarce, my neighbours made every opportunity to get their hands on some especially if that meant eating bugs.

Meanwhile, back in the West, we have more meat than we know what to do with. We could eat meat every day of our lives and not think anything about it. Some people even do this - they call themselves carnivores. They probably get lots of space on public transport too if you know what I mean.

Meat is good and I love eating it. But does our excessive meat consumption come at a cost? If it does, at what cost? Rewind back to what self provisioning is all about - being able to provide for some of your needs for some of the year. How could you do this but with meat?

## Nature's Larder

For tens or even hundreds of thousands of years before this book was written, the main way to get meat on the table was hunting. You could hunt deer, rabbits, antelope, boar, bears, woolly mammoths, whales, seals - anything that was edible and could be fitted around a sharp pointy thing was game - literally.

Then there was fishing - big fish, little fish, sea fish, shellfish. All could be eaten and surplus often preserved in salt, pickled or smoked. Imagine if you could get back there - even just once in a while? Fishing or hunting - man against nature in a never-ending bid for survival. Let's not kid ourselves - life even a hundred years ago was unimaginably harder than it is now. But have we thrown a big baby out with the bathwater?

Here's my approach. I go hunting regularly. I'm fortunate to live where there is plenty of game and plenty of places to hunt. As much as possible, I take home what I kill to eat - it's my way of thanking nature for letting me take a little piece home with me to put in my freezer.

Hunting doesn't fulfil all my family's meat needs - we'd be sick of venison or rabbit otherwise. But it does augment it. Again this is what self provisioning should be.

What about fishing? If that's your thing, great. Sport fishing is a lot of fun but eating what you catch is best (assuming that's legal where you live). In the UK, freshwater fishing tightly protected but sea fishing is a lot freer. In my opinion the best tasting fish are in the sea anyway.

A few hours with a mackerel rod in late summer could give you enough fish for a whole winter. That's free protein right there.

But what if you don't have access to land or guns for hunting and you live miles from the sea and can't fish? What could you do instead?

Try this - think more about where your meat comes from. Could you eat more sustainably grown, free range meat less often? Do you know anywhere you could get game meat? Is there a local fish market that sells sustainably caught sea food?


## A More Sustainable Approach to Eating Meat

I don't believe that going 'meat free' will save the planet any more than cycling to work every day. But there are simple things that you can do to make sure your meat is from sustainable sources.

## 1. Buy Local Meat

In my village there is a rare thing: a local butcher. He sources all his meat from within a short distance of the shop. All his beef is free range, grass fed and from prime beef cattle.

Buy from the supermarket and you're more likely to be eating last week's dairy cow. When I get my turkey at Christmas, it comes from a free-range farm a few miles away. Is that more expensive? Definitely, but we're going for quantity over quality here.

## 2. Go Hunting

You can't get much lower impact than driving out to a forest, shooting a deer, butchering it at home and eating it. Make sure you're doing this legally! Wild meat tastes indescribably better than store bought and is often leaner and higher in protein than farmed meats.

## 3. Eliminate (or reduce) Wastes

When you cook a chicken or a roast a leg of lamb, what do you do with the bones or carcass? There's a log of goodness in the parts we often throw away. Most people (the old me included) don't know how to pick a chicken clean and even fewer know how to make a simple stock from the bones that can then be used for soup. Meat bones make excellent broth or stocks for soups. Offal is a great source of vitamins, iron and other minerals but so much of this is considered 'waste'.

Here's my simple stock recipe:

*Chicken carcass or lamb bone*

*1 stick of celery - chopped*

*1 carrot - cut in half*

*1 onion - in quarters*

*Salt and pepper*

*Water*

Bring all the ingredients to the boil then simmer of 1.5-3 hours. Strain the bones and veg and discard (preferably on your compost heap or food waste bin), keeping the liquid. You can use it straight away, adding chopped vegetables and barley for a Scotch broth or freeze for later use.


## Respect Your Meat - It Died for You

The meat that you eat literally died for you. The least you can do is respect it, make sure it had a good life and use every part of it that you can. It might save the planet, it might not. Either way it's the right thing to do.

# Chapter 7: The Self Provisioner's Crop List

No gardening book would be complete without a crop list. I've read a lot of gardening books and by default, the same number of crops lists. And so it's difficult to know what to add into this process. I've decided however, to include my thoughts on the subject with a few caveats.

1. **This is not an exhaustive list.** It's actually pretty brief because I'm only including crops that I like to grow, and I know work well for the self provisioning gardener. Remember that you are looking to grow crops that will replace a significant part of your grocery needs for a part of the year. Salads and crops that store poorly need not apply.

2. **This is not in any particular order** other than how I've thought of them. I know what works in my garden and what really doesn't. I don't have a greenhouse (artificially forcing plants that can't grow naturally feels more like hydroponics than gardening to me) and if I did, I'd only use it to get plants started off. I live in east central Scotland where we have short growing seasons and long, mild winters.

3. **There are other good crops lists out there (I** especially like the list in *Grow or Die* which is ordered in terms of what is best for survival of a global catastrophe). As with any subject, don't just take my opinion on the subject but read widely. Oh, and try

things for yourself to see what works. This iterative approach is at the heart of self provision gardening.

So, without anything further to add, let's look at my top crops for the self provisioning gardener.

## Potatoes

Although these are sometimes called 'Irish' potatoes, they actually originate from South America and were brought to Europe by English explorers. So not very Irish at all. But potatoes are super as a self provision crop.

They are versatile, easy to grow, easy to store and the flavour of your own home-grown ones vs shop bought is truly mind blowing. If you have the space, grow an 'early' variety (good for boiling, potato salads) and a main crop for roasting, mashing. My main tip would be to avoid the temptation to plant them too close together. This is an easy mistake to make. But potato plants are hungry beasts and will quickly fill above and below ground space. Main crop potatoes should be at least 60 cm (2 feet) between rows and 45 cm (1 ½ feet) between plants.

## Swede

In Scotland, we call these turnips or 'neeps'. English people tell us we're wrong and that turnips are a different vegetable altogether (but then Australians call them Rutabagas so at least we're not that mental). A root crop that is part of the cabbage family, they need early protection from birds and ongoing from caterpillars and slugs. But, once established, they grow quickly and will store over winter in the ground. A touch of frost will improve flavour as the starches in the bulbous roots turn to sugars. I like to roast with carrots but you could also make a Scotch broth (here's my recipe)

Lamb or beef leg bone

2 carrots

½ Swede

1 cup Scotch broth mix of barley, dried peas and lentils (soaked and drained)

1000ml water/vegetable stock

Salt and pepper to taste

Boil together for two to three hours and blend. If you leave overnight in the fridge, the flavours will improve drastically. Stupendous!


## Broad Beans

If I had to choose one vegetable to take with me to a desert island, broad beans would be right up there. Broad (sometimes called fava) beans grow well in cool climates, crop heavily and store well.

You may know broad beans as the rubbery, grey things your Granny used to serve you with mince and potatoes (just me then?). But they are a very versatile vegetable. You can eat the immature pods whole or even make a hummus from the green seeds. The mature seeds store well in the freezer or can be dried and roasted with a little salt for a handy snack.

Beans are legumes - one of their cool tricks is that they 'fix' atmospheric nitrogen down into the soil which gives them food to grow. But - this doesn't mean they'll do well in poor soil. You should still look to incorporate plenty of animal manures and organic matter before sowing.

## Runner Beans

Staying on the bean theme, runner beans are pretty cool too. The immature pods make a lovely summer vegetable. I like my boiled with a little soy sauce. Don't leave them too long or they go coarse and bitter.

The mature seeds when dried, can be used instead of kidney beans but are meatier. To get the best of both worlds, do successive pickings of the green pods and when you've had your fill, let what's left to mature and dry.

You can also store the immature pods - cut them into one-inch lengths and blanche - this means boil for no more than a minute. Then drain, cool and lay out on greaseproof paper so they're not touching. Freeze and when solid, peel them off and put in a bag before putting back in the freezer.

## Pumpkins or Winter Squash

Winter squash is so called, not because it grows in the cold but because it will store right through winter. Pumpkins and squash need lots of space, nutrients and water so be prepared to put the work in.

Living in Uganda, we used to hide the squash plants down in the valley bottom where they mixed with the undergrowth and were hard to spot - a ripe pumpkin was too much temptation for some of my sticky-fingered neighbours! Hopefully your neighbours are a bit more honest.

The best way to grow pumpkins or squash is in 'melon pits' which I learned about from David the Good but actually came from Steve Solomon who learned it from a book about Native American farming. Here's how you do it:

1. Dig a deep pit - as deep as you can - and half fill with fresh manure, kitchen scraps, dead animals, wood ash and urine or a combination of all five.
2. Then put the soil back in the hole. This will create a raised mound.
3. Plant your seeds (or your young plants) into this mound. The roots of the plant will go deep down into the lovely, nutrient rich goodness and give you stonking, big fruit.

I've done this every time I've grown squash or courgette (see next) with excellent results.

Once harvested, certain varieties of squash can store for months in a cool cellar or garage. Make sure you harden the skin off in the sun or a laundry cupboard first for a few days before leaving in a cool, dark and dry place.

## Courgette (Zucchini)

A courgette is just an immature marrow. I say 'just', but it's infinitely better and tastier than its adult form. Let's be real - a marrow is just a big mass of watery tastelessness. "Hey, that was a delicious marrow I ate last night." said no one ever.

Confession time - these didn't make it into my first version of the crop list. I didn't really like courgette. But only because I'd only ever eaten the hydroponically grown fakery from the supermarket. The first time I ate my own courgette fresh from the garden, my mind was blown. Now I can never eat store bought ever again.

You grow them in the same way as pumpkin and winter squash. A good rule of thumb is to pick them when they're a bit bigger than the tip of your thumb to the start of your wrist. Once they get to salami size, they're far too mooshy.

Another good rule is one plant per adult in the home. Otherwise you'll have so many courgettes you'll be eating them all summer. I made this mistake once and ended up giving carrier bags of courgette away to friends and family.

## Onions

One of the most satisfying parts of self provision gardening is not having to buy something for a while because you freaking well grew it yourself. Onions are a great example of this. Onions form the base of so many dishes, adding flavour and bulk. They're easy to grow, store well. Oh, and you can pickle them. They're a self provisioners all-rounder.

I grow my onions from 'sets' which are immature bulbs planted in autumn or early spring. These mature quickly in the short Scottish growing season. Some varieties enjoy being in the cold soil over winter.

To store properly, you need to dry them out. Pull them up and lay them in the sun to dry. This could take up to three weeks. Once the leaves have died back, plait them into attractive braids. Or if you're like me, do the best you can. Keep them hanging somewhere cool and dry and use as you need them.

## Garlic

Garlic makes every meal better. And it keeps the vampires away. Similar to onions, these grow well in cool climates where you get a proper winter. So, they do great in my cold little corner of Scotland. What they don't like is wet feet so plant in a well-drained soil.

I've tried both hardneck (store well) and softneck (don't store as well but a milder flavour). A hardneck variety is my choice now - some of my garlic from a year ago did five to six months in storage.

## Kale

Part of the Brassica (think cabbage) family, kale is a winner on several levels. Firstly, it's one of the most nutritious green vegetables out there. Secondly, it's easy to grow - just keep it well protected when it's young. Third it will continue to grow and give you greens right through a cold winter. I've gone out to the garden, dug down into the snow and harvested wonderful, sweet kale.

The best varieties are the black Tuscan 'Cavolo Nero' types. I've grown a variety called 'Black Magic' which has performed well every time. To encourage constant cropping, grow 6 - 8 plants and cut 2-3 leaves off each plant per harvest.

You can also freeze kale by blanching (see above) and packing into bundles or cubes and freezing.

## Apples

I've eaten apples for as long as I can remember. But I've only eaten them from my own garden for the last few years. The taste cannot be compared.

Apples are one of the most versatile self provisioner crops - and the easiest to grow. You don't even need much space. A nice dessert apple and a cooker on dwarf rootstock will fit in even the smallest allotment or veg plot.

Apples store well and can be made into some incredible preserves including apple butter (think very concentrated, spicy apple sauce), jelly or chutneys and pickles. Oh and cider. And who doesn't like cider?

I personally prefer to make apple jelly. I always add a squirt of lemon juice to the jelly as it boils. I'm not sure why but it makes the whole thing taste wondrous.

## Jerusalem Artichoke

If the world was about to end and I could only choose one crop to save it would be the humble Jerusalem artichoke. Unlike the more refined globe variety, this relative of the sunflowers are grown for their starchy tubers.

The ultimate in low maintenance gardening, plant these in the spring and apart from a little support you can leave well alone. Once the top growth starts to die back, cut down to ground level. The tubers will stay quite happy in the soil over winter. They taste a bit like nutty potatoes with a hint of petrol (nicer than they sound).

A word of caution - eating a lot of these could generate an unwanted, erm, side effect. My wife and I discovered this after having artichoke soup for a starter and roast artichokes with our meal. Explosive.

They can also double up as pig food in emergencies apparently though I'm not sure what that would smell like.


## Make Your Own List

The list above isn't supposed to be exhaustive. But it should give you some ideas. If you're new to growing your own food, start small and simple. As you learn you can start to add in more adventurous crops. You'll also learn what works in your climate and what doesn't. Embrace the failures as well as successes - all of these help you learn how to work your land better.

# Appendix 1: What I Learned About Gardening and Life from Monty Don.

I love a good gift. And I love gardening books. So, when my wife gave me Down to Earth by Monty Don as a present, I was pretty pleased.

This book covers a range of Monty's wisdom on gardening, philosophy and life. It's not your usual gardening book of techniques, tips and a crops list. Instead it's a high-level view of Don's approach to gardening. Which is also his approach to life.

**My Gardening Life**

I was six or seven years old when I begged my Dad to let me have a corner of his garden. I'd borrowed a book on organic vegetable gardening from the public library which I'd poured over for hours. Eventually he gave me my own triangle of dirt at the back of the garage. It was my very own plot to grow and tend. I'd spend hours digging it over, dreaming about what plants I would grow.

Years later, living in Uganda, I ended up with a much larger plot – three or four acres. I had a full-time gardener and turned it from a rain-washed wasteland into a fertile garden of beans, corn, cabbage and peanuts in a few short months. After a few months I had enough food growing to sustain my needs and that of my house staff.

More recently I've picked up where I left off with my gardening. A new house and more land have allowed me to realise my dreams of growing as much of my own food as possible. Access to land for hunting has further improved my lot with wild venison and fowl for the table.

This was where I came across the idea of self provisioning for the first time. Monty's assertion is that self sufficiency - where you rely totally on the land for your needs - is an unrealistic pipe dream. More on that later.

The book taught me three things about the way I garden (and about life in general). Here they are.

## 1. Work With but Don't Force Nature

It's early on a spring morning and I'm looking down in dismay at my frosted potato vines. Thinking I could steal a march on my neighbours and have the first new potatoes of the season, I neglected one consideration – the Scottish weather.

Of course the plants were scorched and brown. Did they recover? Eventually – but any advantage I might have had was lost. If I'd held my patience and waited a few more weeks, I would still have had shining white potatoes – and no cold related scorching.

This is one of the themes through Don's book – don't find against nature. Mainly because she will always win. Instead work with nature and the seasons.

Monty says:

"In the traditional worldview, the 'good' gardener is the one who triumphs over nature…This is nonsense on every level. You need nature more than she needs you. It is not an equal relationship. Serve her well and she will look after you. Abuse her and everyone loses.

Don't plant too early (or too late) and don't try and push natural zones for plants – they won't thank you for it and will perform accordingly."

## 2. Gardening is Therapy

What is the best therapy to improve your mental health? Is it the latest drug? Counselling? Or could it be something simpler and more accessible. Like gardening? Anecdotally, gardening can help improve your mood. I often go out to the garden to decompress and chill. It's amazing how being in that environment can change your mood and frame completely. But there's also a backing in science – gardening really can improve your mood and mental health.

Monty Don is someone who has been outspoken about his struggles with mental health and depression. And although he doesn't spell it out in Down to Earth, it's clear that gardening has been an essential element of his path through life.

If you struggle with stress, anxiety or any kind of mental unease or unwellness, is it time you took up gardening? Too many of us men are struggling with mental health when something as simple as a few hours in the garden each week could make all the difference.

## 3. Ditch Self Sufficiency for Self Provision

Ever since watching The Good Life - a show about a couple who try to live off the land in the London suburbs, I thought the idea of self sufficiency was cool. The idea of being self-reliant on the land - your own land - for all your needs is exciting, attractive. That's true freedom isn't it?

There is a big community around the world of people who want to become self sufficient – not relying on outside help for their basic needs. And while admirable, for most of us, it's either unattainable or impractical. You might see heavily doctored images on the internet that make it look achievable. But it's not.

Which is why I was glad when Monty Don introduced the concept of 'Self Provision' in Down to Earth.

This is the idea that you self provide as much food and produce from your garden as possible without going to the extreme of animal husbandry, home butchery and root cellars.

That's definitely where I want to aim with my own gardening ambitions. Sure, books like Grow or Die are cool and have some great ideas. But with the space and time I have at the moment, I'm more keen to grow great tasting veg that the whole family will enjoy.

Self provision allows me to do that while still playing around with food preserving and storing.

Monty's passion for gardening and horticulture drips from the pages. To read something so beautiful and so engaging from a true master of his craft is a special privilege indeed. Even if you don't enjoy gardening, this should be reason enough for you to read.

But if you're like me and have a lifelong passion for gardening and the outdoors, you'll be doubly enthralled by the passion, wisdom and downright good advice that Monty brings to this, one of the foremost of my gardening book collection.

The Self Provisioner – Neil M White

# Appendix 2: How to Build A Waterless Outdoor Urinal

How do you make a outdoor urinal? And can you make a waterless urinal from recycled materials and things you find lying around the house? Thankfully a simple outdoor toilet/urine recycling system is easy to make, environmentally friendly and cheap.

Every person in the world produces urine. You probably pass between 1.3 and 2 litres of it every day (2 litres is 4.5 pints). Normally you just flush it down the toilet. That might be convenient for you, but the planet hates you for it.

Urine from a healthy person is sterile but if you mix it with ordinary sewage it becomes toxic waste and a proper nightmare to get rid of. So, it would be useful to have a way to dispose of your urine safely and productively wouldn't it? Enter the homemade outdoor waterless urinal.

### Your Urine is an Untapped Resource

Depending on your diet (high protein is best) your pee contains between 12% and 14% nitrogen. This is one of the things that plants need to grow. The problem is that if you urinate directly onto your plants you will burn them. Your urine is just too strong. Oh, and you'll be that weird guy who pees on his garden.

But if you can find a way to treat and 'dilute' your pee, you'd be able to use it as a cheap, and not particularly icky, source of fertiliser. My homemade outdoor urinal safely treats and converts urine into plant food and compost – no waste, no odour. Just plants and piss.

By using ordinary hay (dried grass) to treat the urine, you let it break down in a carbon rich environment. The nitrogen is 'diluted' by the carbon in the dried grass which turns your hot urine into something a whole lot more like compost. After a year you can either dig it out and use on your garden as mulch or add more hay and compost on top to build up layers of well-rotted material.

## How to Make Your Own Waterless Urinal

I'm all about recycling and reusing materials wherever you can. And my waterless urinal design is no different. If you want to make one you will need:

- A length of old hosepipe
- A plastic funnel and tape
- Half an old whisky barrel
- Meadow hay or dried grass
- Homemade or bought garden compost

## Step 1: Make Your Funnel and Hose

Put the hose over the spout of the funnel. You might need to cut the pipe to get a good fit. Secure with tape – strong adhesive duct tape or plumbers' tape is fine. I use T-Rex tape because it has a dinosaur on the packet and sounds cool.

If you intend on actually peeing into the funnel, go as large as possible. This will be how you transport the urine to where you want it: the middle of the hay.

For added filtration of your urine, pierce a few holes in the hose where it will sit in the hay. This will stop your pipe backing up if your flow is too strong.-

## Step 2: Fill Your Whisky Barrel with Hay

Then fill your whisky barrel up with hay. If you don't live in the Highlands of Scotland and can't find whisky barrels lying around, you can use any strong container with holes in the bottom. An old bathtub would work well or a cut down plastic drum.

Fill the barrel with hay. Around 18-25lbs (10 kilos) will be enough for half a barrel but more is fine too. Not enough and it won't have the dilution effect you need. Don't use fresh grass – it will just go slimy and horrible.

Put the hose in the centre of the hay and cover. It should point downwards away from whatever you're going to grow.

## Step 3: Cover Your Homemade Urinal with Compost and Sow Seed

A thin layer of compost on top of the hay will perform two functions. Firstly, it will help minimise any odours from rapidly composting grass. It will also give you a good medium on which to grow your plants. A layer of 5-10 centimetres (2-4 inches) should be enough.

Now your urinal is ready to be sown. What you grow is up to you. If you're a hard-core garden survivalist wild man you could grow vegetables. Or if (like me), your wife has a say, flowers.

The plants you grow will be fed by the nutrients in your urine which are made useful to the plants by the decomposing hay. It's science, Jim but not as we know it.

The contents will settle over time and you may want to top up with more hay and compost after your plants have died back in the winter. If you dig out your barrel, put that lovely nutrient rich stuff on your compost heap. Your veggies will love you for it.

## Top Tips for Your Outdoor Urinal

If urinating in front of your neighbours is a step too far, you could do it in a milk bottle or similar container and transport it to your 'special planter'.

Get your kids involved for a bit of a science lesson. Mine helped build and plant our urinal and had a great time doing it. Maybe 'forget' to tell the neighbour's kids about this one though.

I got the inspiration for this system from '*Liquid Gold: The Lore and Logic of Using Urine to Grow Plants*' by Carol Steinfield which is a *very* comprehensive look at uses for urine. Check out Further Reading for this and more.

# Appendix 3: How to Reconnect with the Land

Note: This is an essay from my blog 'ThisDadDoes.com' and also appears in a similar format in my first book *A Father's Mission*.

Let me start this section with a question: How connected are you to the land? I'm talking about the mucky, gritty stuff that you grow things in. Do you know how to grow and raise crops or trees or do you think that milk comes from cartons and potatoes from the vegetable aisle.

The truth is that our increasingly urbanised population is losing touch with the outdoors and the land in particular. I remember when my son asked me what factory the pork he was eating came from. More and more we've become detached from the land and in particular the way that it produces food for us to eat. But it wasn't always this way.

Rewind 200 years or so and you're in the days before the industrial revolution. You probably live in the country and you definitely don't have electricity, the internet or supermarkets. If you don't grow your own food, you'll die or at least be very poor and reduced to working for others just to eat.

In Europe, farming has been around for at least 4000 years and in other parts of the world for much longer. So your ancestors were raising animals and crops, hunting and foraging for millennia before the recent few decades in which we've lost much of this knowledge. This isn't the case in other cultures however. Living in Uganda I came face to face with a primarily agrarian culture. Until 60 or 70 years ago, Ugandans were totally dependent on farming for survival. This has changed in urban areas but subsistence farming - where you farm primarily for your own use - is still commonplace in rural villages.

Even Ugandan city dwellers have small farms (called shambas) on the outskirts of their city or near their home villages. It's cheaper and easier to grow some crops than buy them in the supermarket or farmers markets. In the village where I lived in the north west of the country everyone grew their own crops and raised their own animals – even me. Farming in Uganda is a family affair with young children working alongside their parents. One farmer who came to help me sow peanuts brought his eight-year-old son to drop the red seed into the small holes he was scraping. Children are given miniature hoes to teach them how to produce food from the land.

This seems like a foreign culture now – of sons and daughters helping to grow the family's food. Farming is done on an industrial scale and food can be bought so cheaply that no-one really has any need to raise their own. The idea of children working in the fields might horrify you. But why? It would have been the expected norm prior to the industrial revolution. Children of rural communities in developed countries still skip school when they are needed to bring in the harvest.

The truth is that we are living in a time of plenty. We don't need to grow our own food because it can be bought for a few pounds at the supermarket. Advanced refrigeration and storage techniques mean that I can eat asparagus from Peru, blueberries from Chile and celery from Spain - all in the same meal. Our shopping habits and demand have created this market where food can be flown by jet to our shores and the farmers still make a profit. My local German discount supermarket sells almost every food I'll ever need (not espresso coffee though – don't get me started).

But this current reality has a caveat. And it's a big one: Although we live in stable and plentiful times, there's no guarantee that this will continue indefinitely. In fact the longer this goes on for, the more likely that we will face real instability. It would only take oil prices to rise due to an unforeseeable conflict or natural disaster and global food prices would skyrocket. And then where would we be?

In Pat Frank's classic post-apocalyptic thriller *Alas Babylon*, the people of fictional Fort Repose are totally unprepared for nuclear disaster. Even though it was expected (the book is set in the mid 1960's) most are shocked when it happens and then attempt to live their lives normally with disastrous consequences. How much more shocked and unprepared would we be in our post-post-cold war times? If this worries you that's probably a good sign. It means you're awake and alert to worst case scenarios. God forbid we ever see anything like this. But if global instability did take hold, would you know how to feed yourself and your family?

A few generations ago, people in the UK were dying from starvation. There wasn't enough food and it was expensive to buy. Over a million Irish and Scots emigrated to America following the great potato famine which destroyed crops as well as lives. Hunger was a regular feature of life. But now we have the opposite problem: obesity. We have access to too much food. And not just junk food.

Our grandparents and great grandparents would barely be able to believe the abundance of foodstuffs we have access to. My own father, who lived through the second world war, remembers the first time he saw a banana. He was 10. Now bananas are a few pennies each.

We live in a time of plenty – don't let anyone tell you otherwise. But will that continue indefinitely? There is a type of cognitive bias called 'continuity bias' which means that we expect the current status quo to remain indefinitely. Whatever has happened will keep happening right?

But that's flawed thinking. The captain of the Titanic was famously quoted as saying he'd never been shipwrecked or even been close to being shipwrecked. Tragically, we know what happened to him. People investing in mortgage bonds in the run up to the '07/08 financial crash thought the housing market was a safe bet because it had never nose-dived before. Oh, how wrong they were too.

Nicholas Nassim Taleb's 'Black Swan' event is something that no-one sees coming because they think it's impossible. But how stable is our society and more importantly, our food supply?

Right now, our supply of food is totally dependent on oil. Synthetic fertilisers, farm machinery, delivery vehicles, supermarkets – all need one thing to produce: oil. Which is great. I mean we have total control over all of our oil and none of it comes from unstable places like the Middle East and West Africa, does it?

Globalisation means that our national economies are caught up with the economies of several different nations and continents.

It wouldn't take much to cut global oil production significantly – think something along the lines of the 1956 Suez Crisis when the Suez Canal was closed to shipping from October 1956 to March 1957. Food prices skyrocket and it becomes a challenge just to put food on the table. Are you ready for that altogether possible scenario? While our recent times have been stable and peaceable, there is no guarantee that this will continue indefinitely. Like a roulette wheel that seems stuck on red, it will switch to black at some stage.

## The Tree Stump Philosopher

"Daddy, what are you doing?" My son sidled over cautiously.

"Digging this stump out." I replied breathlessly. "Want to help?"

The tree – a planted yew - had hard wiry roots and a large, flat root plate. I'd dug a trench about three feet in diameter and was starting to dig and lever up the heavy stump. We'd only moved to the new house a few weeks ago but I wasted no time doing some clearance work on the largely neglected garden. I needed this stump out as I plan to convert the area to a grass lawn for the purposes of football, rugby and tickle fights. But in the meantime, I wanted the land for the first crop of potatoes, beans and turnips.

Before moving I'd longed to live in the country. I'd grown up an urban kid and settled in Glasgow - Scotland's biggest city - when I was in my early 20's. In the limited space and light of the city, growing my own food on any real scale was out of the question.

As I was digging, I thought to myself: How many young men my age or boys my son's age would know how to dig up a stump like this? A few generations ago, most Dads would have been able to clear a plot of ground ready for cultivation. But now I'm in the minority. How do you cultivate (oh dear!) this knowledge. I'm fortunate in that I had a Dad who was a keen gardener. Much of the basics I've learned from him. But if you're less confident when it comes to growing your own food, where do you start? And does it even matter?

## Why Living From the Land Matters

Knowing how to grow and survive from the land is something that is an inherent part of our culture and past. If we lose it it is gone forever. Books and learning can help but are a poor substitute for the way I learned – standing at my father's elbow as he showed me how to dig a plot, plant vegetables and watch them grow into something I wanted to eat. Is this really that important?

It doesn't matter if your heritage is from the Siberian steppes, northern Europe or east Africa, your ancestors depended on the land for their food. Mine were almost certainly farmers back in ancient times, raising animals and crops to feed themselves. My more recent ancestors were farmers too. There is a strong heritable link between you and the land. If you've lost it, isn't it time you got it back?

The best way to teach yourself about growing your own food is to start now and experiment. Gardening books are great but eventually you'll need an iterative approach. That means you learn by doing. These days YouTube provides a wealth of gardening advice - good and bad. There are also a number of excellent books which will give you an insight into how to grow food with minimal outside inputs. I'd recommend you start with *Grow or Die: The Good Guide to Survival Gardening* by David The Good and his prequel *Compost Everything* is also excellent. He does have a US focus but provides plenty for a Northern European like me to think about when it comes to crop selection and garden layout. David The Good's advice is to to master growing high calorie foods and in particular root crops before graduating to more complex or delicate veggies.

A more international (and considerably more in depth) approach comes from Steve Solomon's *Gardening When it Counts: Growing Food in Hard Times*. Solomon lives in the Australian island of Tasmania but originates from the United States. His focus is more on temperate climates than David The Good's sub-tropical bias. Conventional gardening books and television programmes have some value but often their techniques are too advanced or complicated for the average time-strapped Dad who just wants to learn how to grow things he can eat.

## Return on Investment – Your Wealth is in the Soil

You've probably heard this asked: 'What's the return on investment on that?'. It's normally used to justify (or otherwise) some type of activity. If you value your time, you already care about return on investment even if you've never called it that before. It's a fancy way of saying 'Is this worth my time'? Something with a high ROI (return on investment) has a big benefit from little input.

So, what's the ROI on learning how to grow your own food? Here's one way of looking at it: It's a poor return on investment. I can a get a whole sack of potatoes for the same price as washing one of my cars. So why would I spend hours outside growing my own? The supermarket vegetable aisle holds more delicious and genetically perfect produce than I could grow in a lifetime.

What if this misses the point completely? The point being that growing your own food isn't about saving money on your grocery bill. It's about learning (or relearning) a near forgotten skill that your ancestors took for granted. As you learn and experiment you use that knowledge to create something (yummy food) ex nihilo – out of nothing. Imagine that look in your children's eyes when you show them their first swelling pumpkin or pluck a carrot from the loose sandy soil.

Reconnecting with the land isn't about the destination – in this case having food to eat. It's about the journey; the process you'll go on with your kids; the delight in their eyes and the inevitable disappointment of failed crops. Those are lessons worth learning for now and for the future – whatever it may bring. When the end result is reconnecting with a forgotten past coupled with possible future survival, that return outstrips the time invested a hundred-fold.

A dear friend of mine and agricultural visionary used to say this:


"Your wealth is in the soil."

He meant that everything we need to eat can come from the land and that the soil is a precious life giving super-organism. It's time we reconnected and got our hands dirty.

## How To Use Your Garden to Teach About Life

My favourite part of coming home from boyhood summer holidays was seeing how much my vegetable patch had grown. One year was extra exciting: It was the first year I'd grown radishes. As we pulled into the drive, I bounded out of the car and round to the back garden. My small allotment was like a jungle and the radish leaves were ginormous!

I started pulling to see what size they had grown to. But I was quickly disappointed as I saw that they were all small and deformed little morsels. I'd forgotten to thin out the small plants which meant the crop was a failure. I probably cried – I don't really remember. Being a farmer at any age is tough but 7 years old is an especially emotional time in your life.

But I learned 2 things. Firstly, always thin out your seedlings or you'll cry. And secondly, sometimes life has bitter disappointment. Things don't always go your way. There aren't always bulbous radishes waiting for you. But you can come back stronger and wiser than before. Don't kid yourself that none of this matters. It does. It matters very much, both now and for the future.

I'm no doomsday prepper, but that doesn't mean I don't believe in being prepared for whatever the future brings. A cursory glance at the history books suggests our time of relative peace is on borrowed time. What comes next? I don't know – but at least I won't go hungry.

## To the Fields!!

Ok, so I stole that line and changed it from the 1990's movie *Robin Hood: Prince of Thieves*. But I do seriously hope that you've been inspired by what you've read in this essay. You don't need much land to start growing your food. But what you do need is the motivation and perseverance to cope with the 'leafy radishes' that will come your way. Approach as a student and you'll become the master.

# Appendix 4: A Father's Mission: Introduction

What is a father's mission in our modern age? As our world becomes more connected, more turbulent and more violent - is the role of the father under threat?

I'm writing these words on the evening of the London Parliament terror attacks. The stability and relative peace that our own fathers enjoyed is coming to an end. We now live in an age of uncertainty: economic, social, political.

In this age of uncertainty, the role of the father is changing. Your role is changing. And while some of these changes are good, not all change is good. Not all change will benefit you or the children you are trying to raise.

Imagine what the role of the father will be in another ten or twenty years. Will it continue to be a positive influence on children? Or are you at the threshold of being culturally side lined.

You Matter Now More than Ever

This book is about you. You might not know it but when I was writing and putting it together I imagined that I was writing it especially for you. We don't know each other very well but by the time you're finished this short book, we will.

This book is about you and your journey to be a better father. I hope it's a journey we're on together. And if it's not a journey we're on together, it's my wish that we soon will be. If you cruise the pages of this book, you'll see a big focus on you. Y-O-U. That's not a mistake. This isn't a parenting book. This is a book on fatherhood and the elements that make up a successful, driven, committed, loving and protecting Dad. All of those traits come from you.

This is what I truly believe: to become a better father you must become a better man. That's not a criticism - we all have different starting points. What is important is the journey you're taking to become a better man. And therefore, a better father.

What is your motivation to become a better Dad? My motivation is simple: Dads matter more in our modern times than ever. We live in a time when pornography, junk food and wall to wall entertainment is on tap. Our kids will grow up with near permanent connection to the World Wide Web. And while that's positive in some ways, in others it can be a negative influence. It's our responsibility to raise our kids right and to pass on our values onto them.

Why? Because it will probably save their lives. Recent studies have shown that kids who have an involved Dad at home are less likely to:

- Commit suicide

- Drop out of school

- Get pregnant before eighteen

- End up in prison or juvenile detention

Here's the thing: there are no quick fixes to personal improvement. There's no sachet of 'Instant Better Dad - just add hot water'. It's a slow, hard grind. It takes work - more work than you'd have ever imagined. But if you're up for the challenge then this is the right book for you.

'Why bother?' I hear the less committed ask. Turn on your TV and you're bombarded with images of deadbeat or 'Star Wars Dads' who'd rather sit and play computer games or watch live streaming Sci-Fi repeats than put the work in to improve their lives and the lives of those around them.

This book is the antidote to that style of fatherhood.

I must admit that this book has transformed from a short 'best of' my blog - ThisDadDoes.com - into something deeper and stronger than I'd ever imagined. It's been a crystallisation of my understanding of what our generation of fathers need now more than ever. Is the book's subject matter diverse? You bet. I'll happily jump from spirituality to easy-to-cook recipes. But there's a method to this madness - to be a good Dad you must be skilled and competent in a range of disciplines and skills.

## Six Pillars for Strong Fatherhood in Our Modern Times

I've divided this book into six parts or 'pillars'. These six pillars form the foundations of strong fatherhood. But they also complement each other. In the same way that a series of pillars keep a roof or a ceiling up, these pillars form six areas of your life that are critical to becoming a strong father.

These pillars are:

1. A Father's Mission

2. Mental Strength

3. Spirituality and Self Control

4. The Knowledge

5. The Outdoors

6. Fitness and Physical Health

All of these disciplines have individual value but when put together they begin to shape you into the father you want to be.

Some of these will challenge you, but at the same time I hope you are comforted. What do I mean by that? I want you to see that you're already doing a good job as a Dad and that it might only take a few small adjustments to bring your life back into focus.

**How to Use this Book**

You'll get the best experience from this book if you start at the beginning and read it all the way through once. You'll find practical advice and ideas on nearly every page. But I'd also encourage you to take time to read a second time and focus on the chapters that you feel you need most work and attention. If something inspires you, highlight it and save it for later.

At the end of most chapters you'll find an 'Action' for you to do. Knowledge without application is worthless, but we'll get to that. I wrote this book so that you would enjoy reading it. Find a quiet place where you won't be distracted, turn your phone off and focus.

Breathe.

Now let's begin.

# Further Reading

I hope you've enjoyed reading The Self Provisioner. In writing this book I have stood on the shoulders of gardening giants. Many of the books in this list I have referenced directly, others deserve your attention and reading time though haven't quite made it into the final edit of this book. Either way, add these to your reading list and let the ideas flow.

*Grow or Die: The Ultimate Guide to Survival Gardening*

David the Good

*Compost Everything: The Guide to Extreme Composting*

David the Good

*Down to Earth: Gardening Wisdom*

Monty Don

*How to Grow More Vegetables*

Jim Jeavons


*A Father's Mission: Strong Fatherhood in Our Modern Times*

Neil M White


*Gardening When it Counts: Growing Food in Hard Times*

Steve Solomon


*Gardening without Work: For the Aging, the Busy, and the Indolent*

Ruth Stout


*Liquid Gold: The Lore and Logic of Using Urine to Grow Plants*

by Carol Steinfield


*The MeatEater Fish and Game Cookbook*

Steven Rinella

# Acknowledgements

It's important for me to take time to thank a few people who have helped make this book possible. Firstly, thank you to Monty Don who first led me to the idea of self provisioning. It was this term that crystallised a concept that already existed in my own mind.

Thanks also to those who have supported me through the process of writing this book - M, a constant source of encouragement, Thor who always believes in my ideas, David - for telling me early on that he was looking forward to reading this book before it was even half written.

A big thanks to Matt for his excellent cover designs and knowing how I wanted the cover to look even before I did. You've created something truly unique.

And for Mike - without you I'm not sure I would have started writing again. It's been a good decision. You taught me to take it word by word.

## About the Author

Neil M White is a father, author and follower of Christ. He lives in rural Scotland with his wife and three children. When not working on his next project he enjoys time in his Self Provision garden or hunting.

# By the Same Author

*A Father's Mission: Strong Fatherhood in Our Modern Times*

By Neil M White

A Father's Mission is one of the most important books on fatherhood to be released this year. A Father's Mission will teach you how to become a better father. And a better man.

Neil M White, author of A Father's Mission has reached thousands of men through his writing. He has one mission - to be a better man and father: a dad who does more.

By applying the concepts explained in A Father's Mission, you will become motivated to excel at your own father's mission. You will become healthier, fitter, more confident. Your relationship with your children will improve.

Each chapter contains real world examples from the author's experience as well as actions for you to take at the end of each chapter.

By applying this short but valuable book, you will become a better man.

You will become a better father.

Are you ready for your father's mission?